GRAPHICA²

THE WORLD OF *MATHEMATICA* GRAPHICS

GRAPHICA 2: THE WORLD OF *MATHEMATICA*® GRAPHICS

THE PATTERN OF BEAUTY: THE ART OF IGOR BAKSHEE

SERIES EDITOR AND CREATIVE DIRECTOR: JOHN BONADIES

WOLFRAM
MEDIA

Graphica 2: The World of Mathematica Graphics
The Pattern of Beauty: The Art of Igor Bakshee

Published by:

Wolfram Media, Inc.

100 Trade Center Drive

Champaign, IL 61820-7237, USA

email: info@wolfram-media.com

web: www.wolfram-media.com

ISBN: 1-57955-010-X

www.graphica.com

For information on licensing *Graphica* images, visit **www.graphica.com/permissions** or send email to **permissions@graphica.com**.

Artlandia, Inc.

2015 Barberry Circle

Champaign, IL 61821-5862, USA

email: artlandia@artlandia.com

web: www.artlandia.com

Credits:
Pattern designs: Igor Bakshee
Art/Creative direction: John Bonadies
Editorial: David Gehrig, Carrie Driscoll
Image preparation: Malgorzata Zawiślak
Publishing management: Allan Wylde
Production management: Judith Quinlan

Printed in China

INTRODUCTION

It seems so easy for nature to produce forms of great beauty—as so often imitated in art. But how does nature manage this? And must we be content with just imitating nature? Or can we perhaps capture whatever fundamental mechanism nature uses to produce the forms it does, and use this mechanism directly for ourselves?

My work in science has led me to the conclusion that for the first time in history, we are finally now at the point where this has become possible. And the key lies in the idea of computer programs. For a computer program, like a natural system, operates according to definite rules. And if we could capture those rules we should be able to make programs that do the kinds of things nature does.

But in fact we can do vastly more. For nature must follow the laws of our particular universe. Yet programs can follow whatever laws we choose. So we can in effect make an infinite collection of possible universes, not just our particular universe.

In the past, however, it has seemed difficult to get programs to yield anything like the kind of richness that we typically see in nature. And when one hears of images made by programs, one tends to think of rigid lines and simple geometrical figures. But what my work in science suggests is that people have created programs with too much purpose in mind: they have tried to make sure that their programs are set up to achieve specific goals that they can foresee.

But nature—so far as we know—has no goals. And so the programs it runs need not be chosen with any particular constraints. And what my work in science has shown is that programs picked almost at random will often produce behavior with just the kind of complexity—and sometimes beauty—that we see in nature. All that is necessary is that we go beyond the narrow kinds of programs whose behavior we, as humans, can readily foresee.

When I created *Mathematica* my goal was to build an environment in which one could easily set up programs of essentially any kind. And indeed the language that underlies *Mathematica* is based on concepts more general and more fundamental than even those of standard logic or mathematics. And by using these concepts it is possible to create programs that correspond to the kinds of rules that seem to operate in nature—or in anything like nature.

In fact, with the *Mathematica* language, remarkably simple programs can often produce pictures of such intricacy and unexpected detail that one would never imagine that they could ever have been made just by following any set of rules.

Sometimes the pictures one gets remind one of some familiar system in nature. And sometimes they look like the creations of a human artist. But often they are something different. They have parts reminiscent of nature. And parts that one could imagine being created by human artists. But then they have unexpected elements, like nothing seen before, together with a vast range of details far beyond what any unaided artist could ever produce.

And this is the essence of the images in *Graphica*.

—Stephen Wolfram
scientist and creator of *Mathematica*

WHAT IS *MATHEMATICA*? *Mathematica* is the tool used to create all of the images in this and other *Graphica* books. *Mathematica* is a software system—an environment for technical computing—originally designed by Stephen Wolfram as a tool for exploring ideas in science, technology, and elsewhere. *Mathematica* was first released in 1988, and in the years since that time it has become the tool of choice for well over a million scientists, engineers, financial analysts, students, and others. *Mathematica* has been used to design airplanes, to analyze stock markets, to manage fisheries, to discover important new science and mathematics, to solve innumerable homework exercises—and also to create art.

As its name suggests, *Mathematica* is built on mathematics, but mathematics interpreted in its broadest—and oldest—sense. *Mathematica* incorporates vastly more facts about algebra, trigonometry, calculus, and other fields of traditional mathematics than any human has ever known or probably ever will know. And it can use these facts to do in seconds calculations that would take humans months or years to do themselves. But the essence of *Mathematica* is its language.

It is not a language like English or French that has been built up haphazardly through centuries of use. It is a language that was designed from the start to provide a clear and precise way of communicating ideas—and a way that could be understood by a computer. Computer languages typically specify the operations in a rather literal and low-level way, most often giving quite explicit procedures for how data should be moved around inside the computer. But *Mathematica* is essentially unique among languages in common use in that it operates at a much higher level—with a much closer correspondence to normal human thinking.

All sorts of people use *Mathematica*, to do all sorts of things. Sometimes people use *Mathematica* like a calculator—asking it mathematical or other questions and letting it use its internal capabilities to work out the answer. Sometimes people use *Mathematica* like a notepad—to record and organize their thoughts and ideas. And sometimes people use *Mathematica* and its language to specify ways to create forms of all kinds—not just formulas and text, but also pictures and sounds. It is the implications of *Mathematica* as a tool for creating visual forms that the *Graphica* series explores.

MATHEMATICA BECOMES AN ARTIST'S TOOL With Wolfram Research's flagship product being based on higher mathematics, it might seem like an intimidating task for an art director to develop an effective visual communications identity. After all, mathematical imagery has traditionally been limited to stodgy charts, tables, and cryptic diagrams. But the graphics capabilities of *Mathematica* have instead allowed us to communicate our product and our company in a way that is both visually intriguing and distinctive.

Nor were we alone in using *Mathematica* to create interesting designs. A collection of graphic images included as a "Graphics Gallery" in the second edition of *The Mathematica Book* in 1991 inspired many users to take a closer look at *Mathematica*'s visualization tools. As a result, a proliferation of strange and interesting graphics began coming across my desk from all over the world.

And from the beginning, these images have not been only utilitarian or scientific. Many who use *Mathematica* in research or education have also come to use it as an artistic tool for their private enjoyment. There are also a growing number of creative people, without any formal training in science or math, who are beginning to experiment with *Mathematica* in their design work. And by now *Mathematica* has been used for set design, special effects in animation, textile design, sculpture, and architecture. And no doubt there are a host of other applications that we are yet to hear about.

Many times I have had the experience of showing these images to people who do not have a deep understanding of mathematics or science. And almost always their reaction has been a strange combination: initially an emotional, aesthetic response, followed by analytical curiosity. To our surprise and delight at Wolfram Research, this kind of reaction has been widespread in many communities.

The graphics in this volume demonstrate intricate connections between art, science, and mathematics that have been made possible by the advent of *Mathematica* as an artist's tool. I hope you find them as I did—unlike anything you have ever seen before. Their mixture of the familiar and the unknown, the algorithmic and the intuitive, has given me the exciting feeling of being present at the birth of a new art form.

—John Bonadies

ix

THE BEAUTY OF RANDOM WORLDS This book originated from my search for a general formula for creating beauty from randomness—a transformation perhaps more appropriate for alchemy than algorithm. On a more pragmatic level, I have also searched for ways to generate beautiful images using the computer, and—more pragmatic still—for an algorithmic means to generate attractive patterns and designs *en masse*, thereby providing a human designer with an inexhaustible source of inspiration.

Sadly, I must report that the alchemistic side of this search has met with as little success as its historic predecessors; a single formula for beauty is as elusive as the legendary "philosopher's stone" that could transmute lead to gold. However, completing the analogy, the search has brought us closer to understanding the canons of artificial pattern generation. It has also provided a wealth of practical recipes incorporated into *Artlandia*, a *Mathematica*-based software application for creative graphic design. In the "What Makes an Attractive Image?" section at the end of this book, I give a few examples of *Artlandia* in action.

The key is to strike the right balance between regularity and randomness. Neither perfect regularity nor pure randomness can make an attractive pattern. A pattern that is completely regular is as visually lifeless as a sheet of blank graph paper. Yet an image containing too much randomness becomes too "busy;" there seems to be a correlation in our minds between complexity and randomness. A degree of orderliness seems to be required for the human eye to make its way through the image, but too much orderliness renders it static and uninteresting.

The orderliness can arise either from a symmetry of the overall image or its parts, or from traces—even subtle ones—of recognizable shapes in the image. The order can be brought about by a mathematical formula or deterministic (nonrandom) part of the drawing algorithm. Various random transformations can also add some visual interest.

Conversely, when the underlying algorithm for the image is stochastic (random), a level of orderliness can be brought about either by the dynamics of the process itself—as it happens, for example, in the chaotic phenomena—or imposed externally. This can be done by rounding the coordinates of shapes to a certain grid, repeating certain random components, operating on random parts in a deterministic way, and by any of countless other methods.

The images in this book explore the unlimited universe of ideas and techniques that balance order and randomness in a controlled proportion, as managed by a practical tool that lets the artist carefully enhance one over the other, just as a chef adds spices to his masterpiece pinch by pinch. One of the examples at the end of this book shows how adding carefully controlled randomness metamorphoses a static image into something that gratifies the eye.

So far I have spoken of randomness as if there were only one kind. There are actually many different sorts of random processes, which are characterized by their power spectra, or how such a random signal would look if fed to an oscilloscope. The most common of these random processes are often colloquially referred to by names of colors, since the color prism was historically the first apparatus for spectral analysis. Of course, such color labels refer to the spectral properties of each process and should not be confused with the use of any specific colors in the images.

The simplest random process is totally uncorrelated and has the flat power spectrum. It is "colorless" and is therefore called the "white" noise. Random processes which are time- or space-correlated and therefore possess a non-flat power spectrum are called "colored." Common examples include the "pink" noise (also called the "flicker" or $1/f$-type fluctuations) and the "random-walk"

White $1/f$ (flicker) $1/f^2$ (random walk)

$(1/f^2)$ fluctuations. The idea of using the flicker-type sequences in pattern design came from Professor T. Musha of Teikyo Heisei University, whose other applications of such processes include the architectural $1/f$ design in Okinawa which appeared in April, 1998 (see http://home.ksp.or.jp/yuragi). A few graphical comparisons of random sequences with different spectral characteristics are depicted at the end of this book.

In all my design efforts, I was fortunate enough to receive advice from textile manufacturers, first in Japan, and later in the United States. I considered this advice as the authoritative judgment on whether a given idea or algorithm did indeed bring about an attractive pattern. In fact, the acceptance of a design for production in fabrics has always been the ultimate criterion for attractiveness and usefulness. This "natural selection" process has helped to shape the scope of images for this book and hone *Artlandia* as a practical tool.

AUTHOR'S ACKNOWLEDGMENTS   I gratefully acknowledge the contributions of Dr. Toshimitsu Musha, with whom I had the pleasure of collaborating closely for several years during my work in Japan. His hospitality made my work and stay in Japan both productive and enjoyable.

Of course, the entire project would not have been possible without *Mathematica*. With its peerless combination of a powerful programming language and symbolic, numeric, and graphical capabilities, *Mathematica* provided a uniquely efficient environment for research and development of new approaches and techniques. I wish to thank my colleagues at Wolfram Research for creating such an outstanding software system. I am also grateful to Stephen Wolfram for his encouragement and support of my artistic endeavors, and more specifically, for contributing ideas for several cellular automata images.

My gratitude also goes to John Bonadies, whose creative talent brought forth this book from the chaos of individual images. I also wish to thank David Gehrig for his patient assistance with the text.

Last, but not least, I am indebted to many textile designers, stylists, and other product developers in America and Japan who have provided and continue to provide their encouragement, insights, and innumerable helpful comments on my designs.

— Igor Bakshee

GALLERY

2

6

7

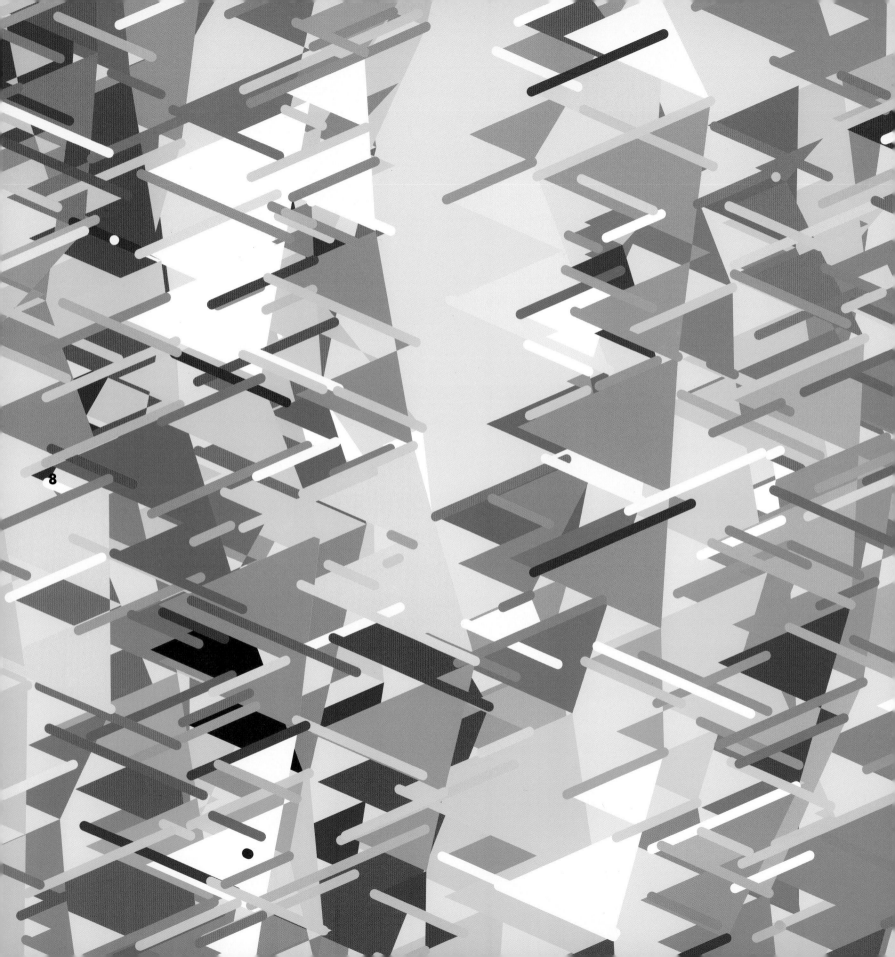

9

10

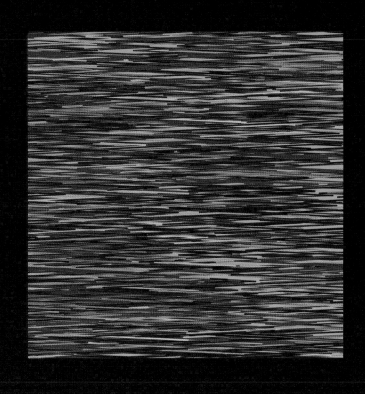

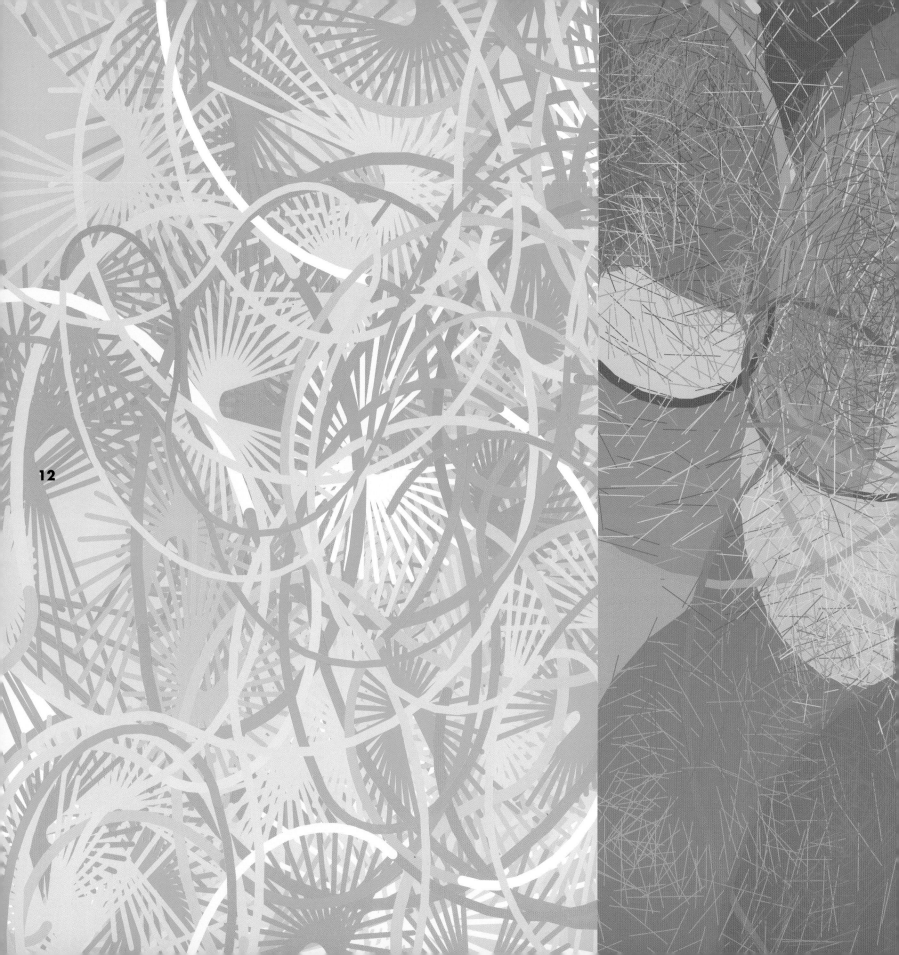

12

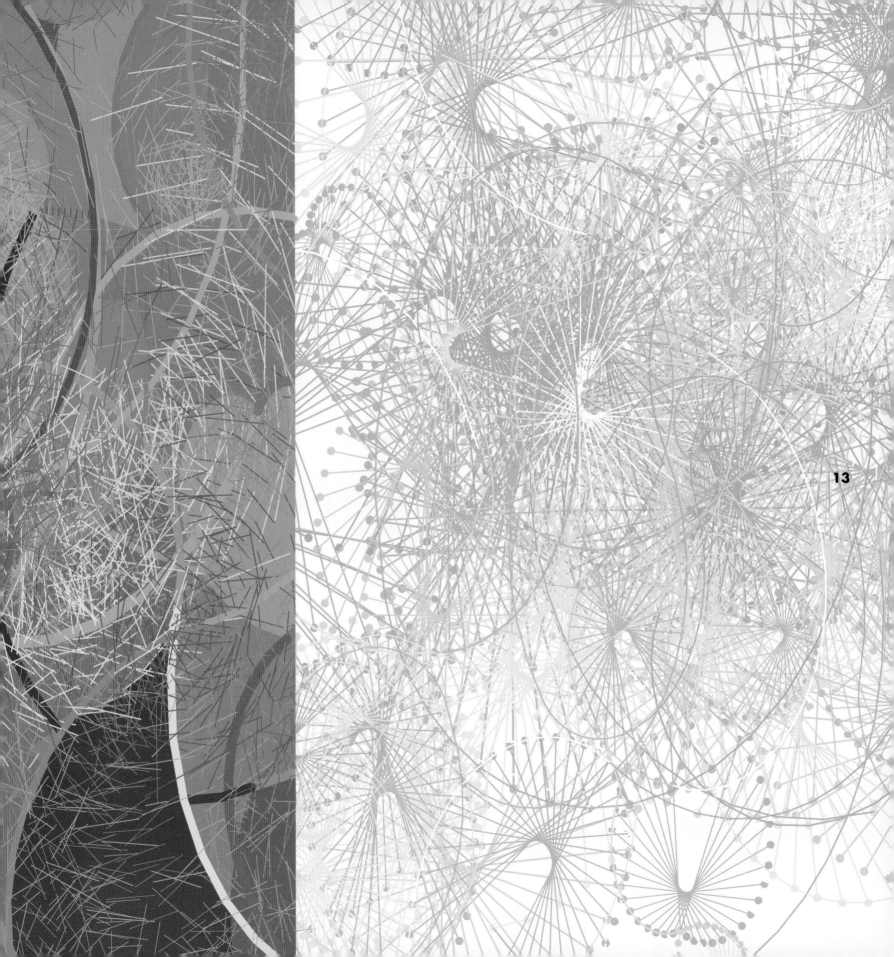

13

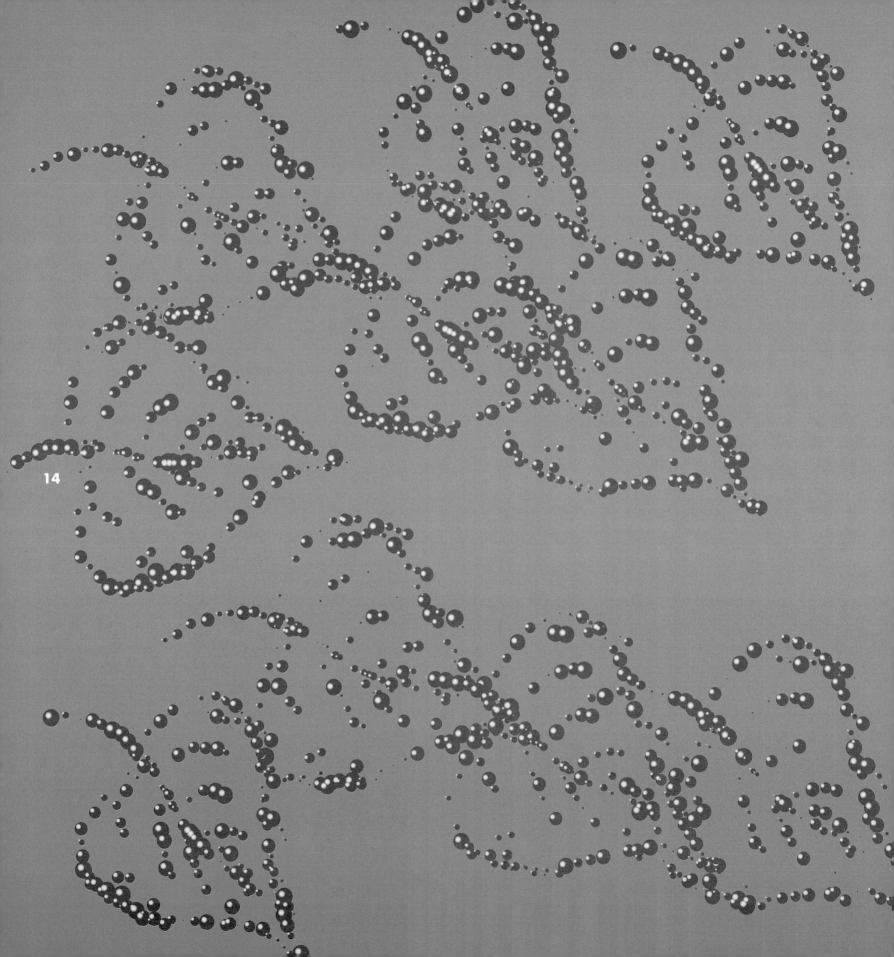

16

17

18

19

20

21

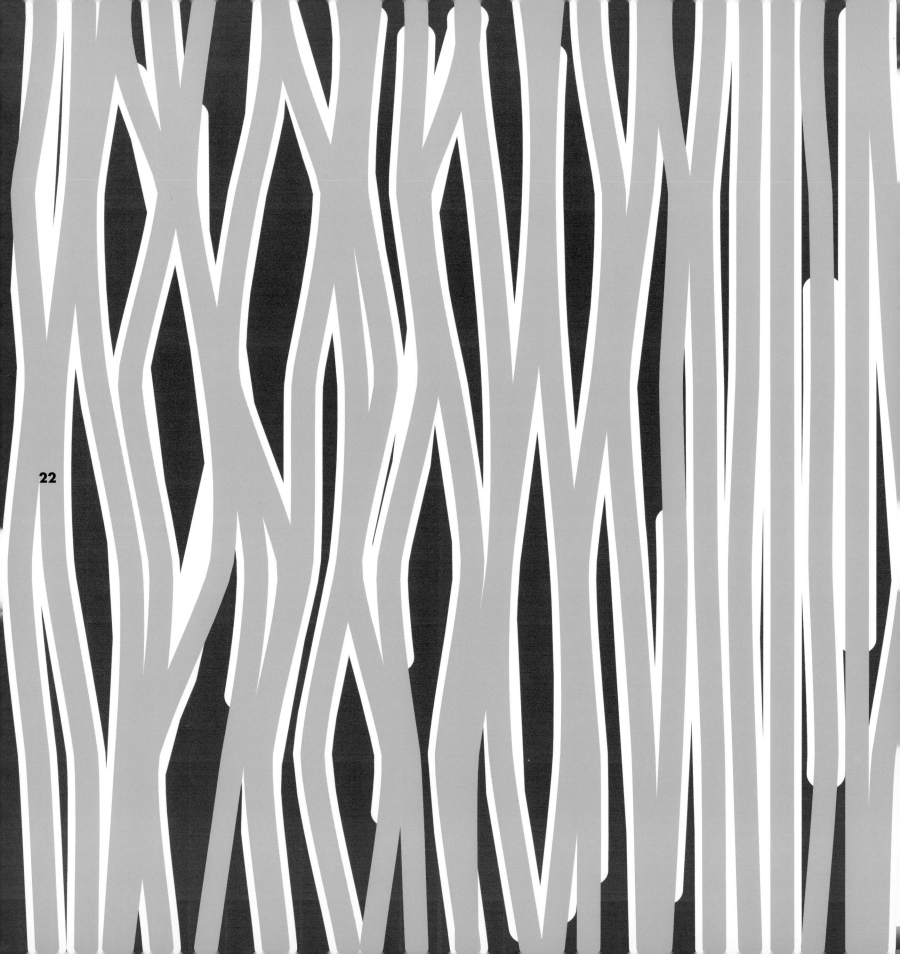
22

23

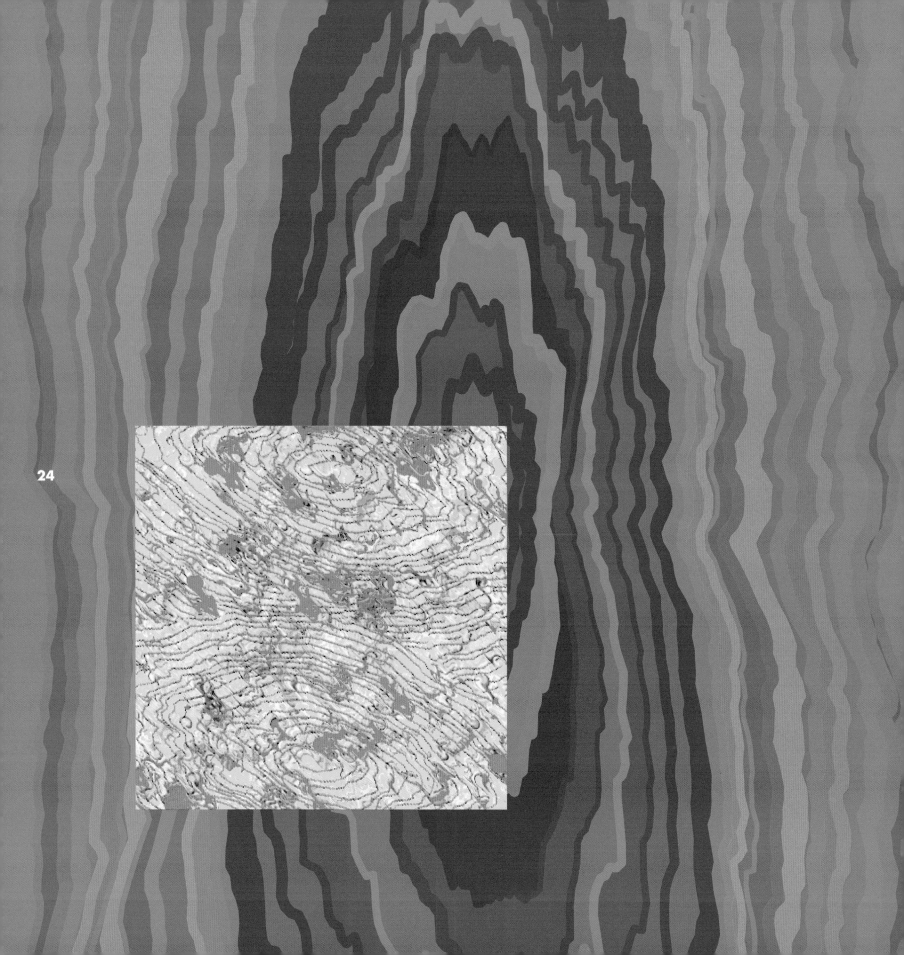

24

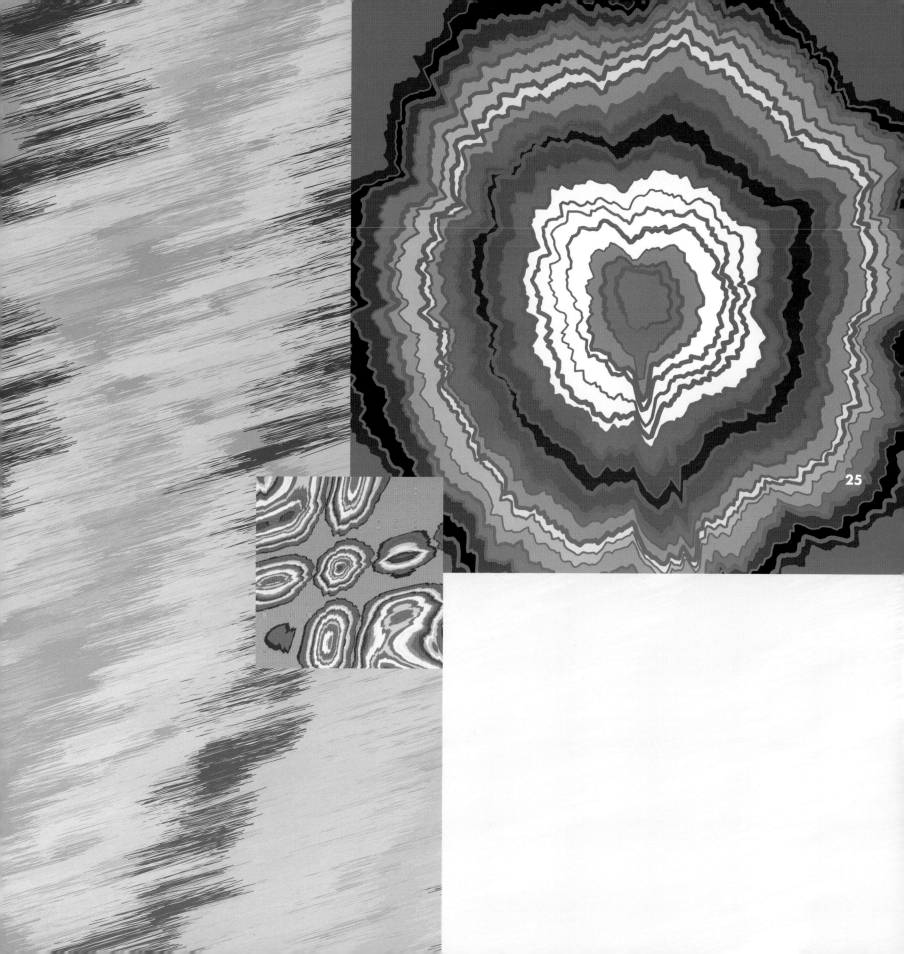

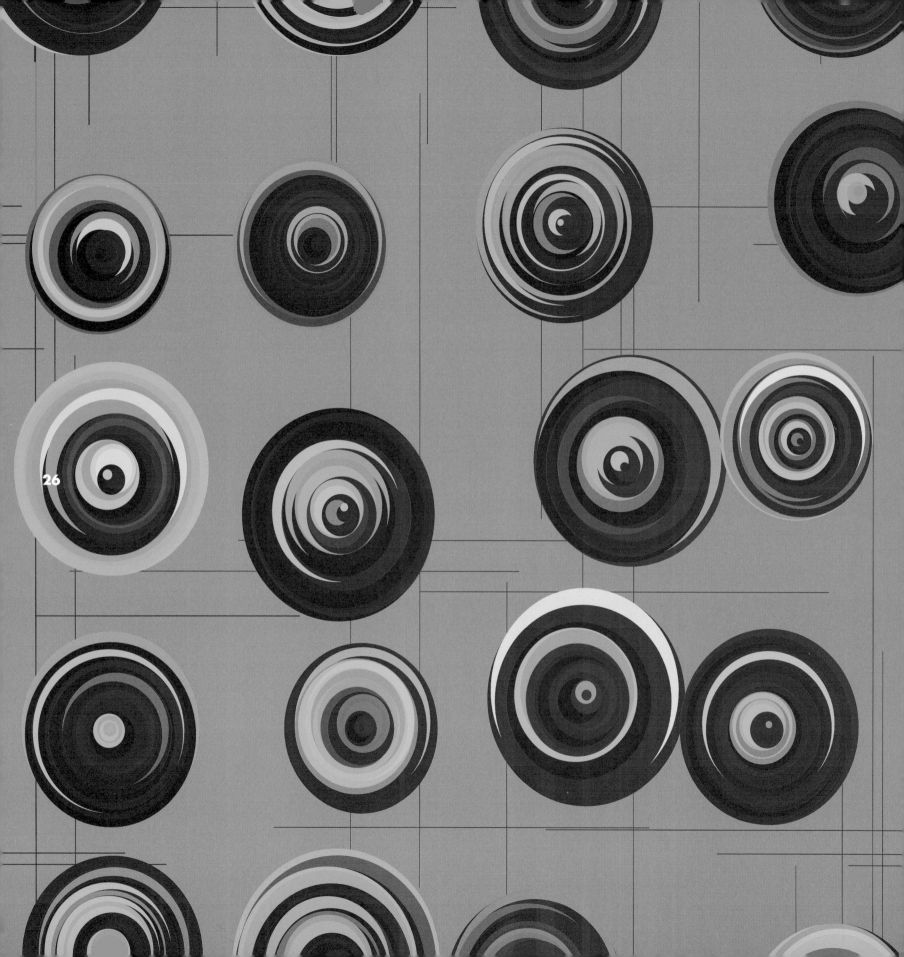

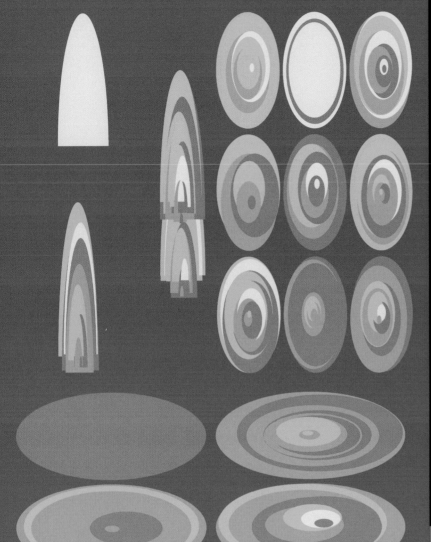

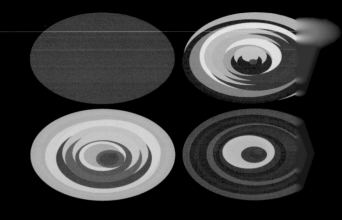

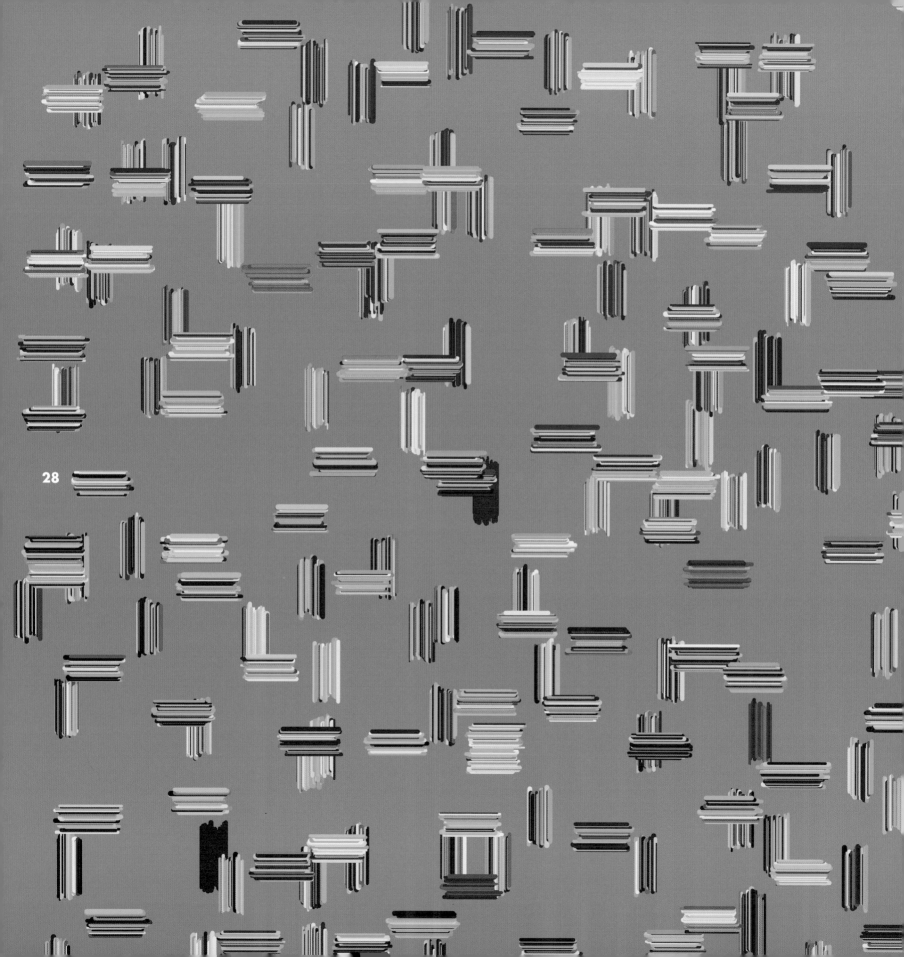

28

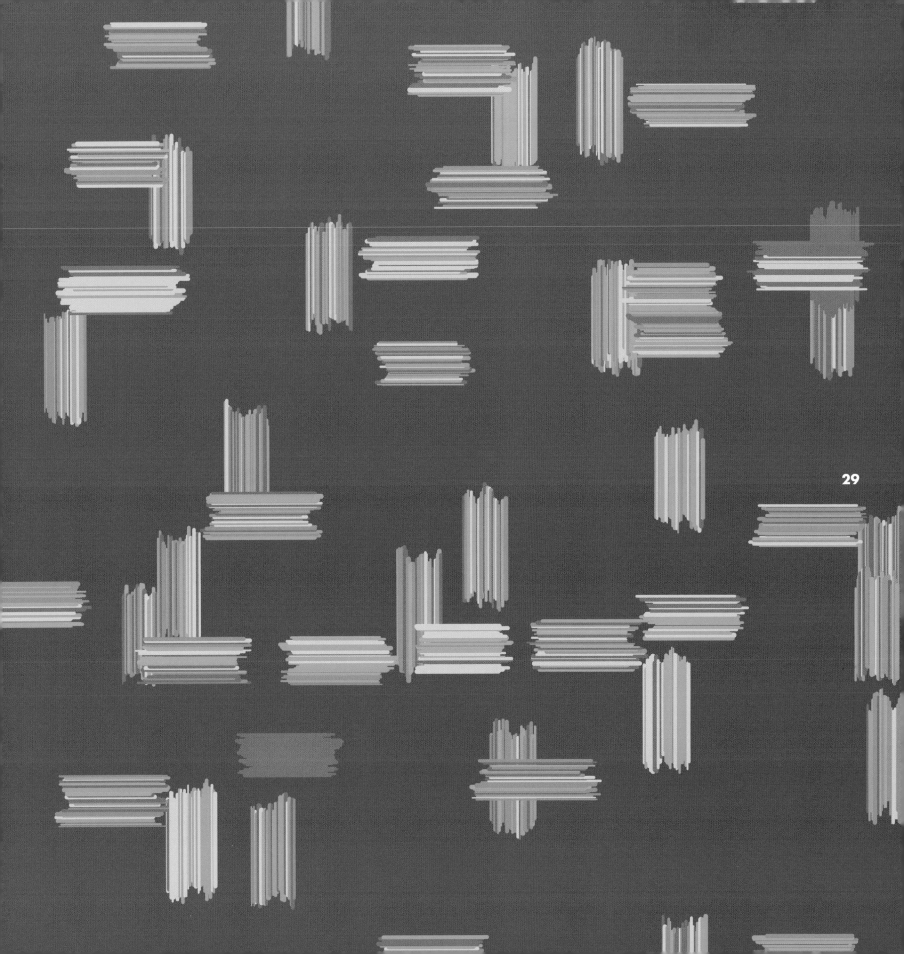

29

30

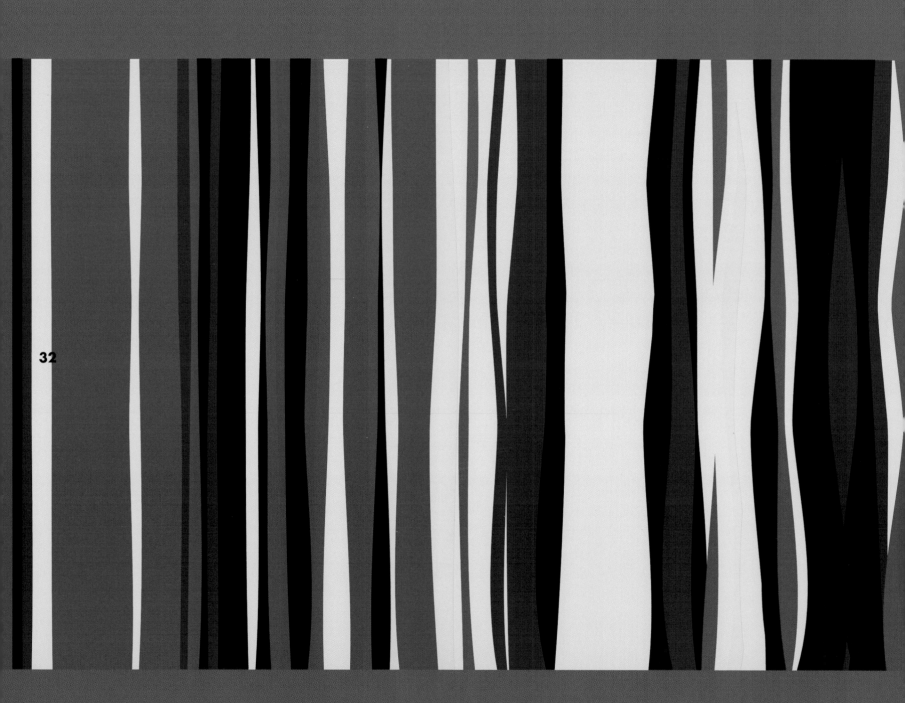

32

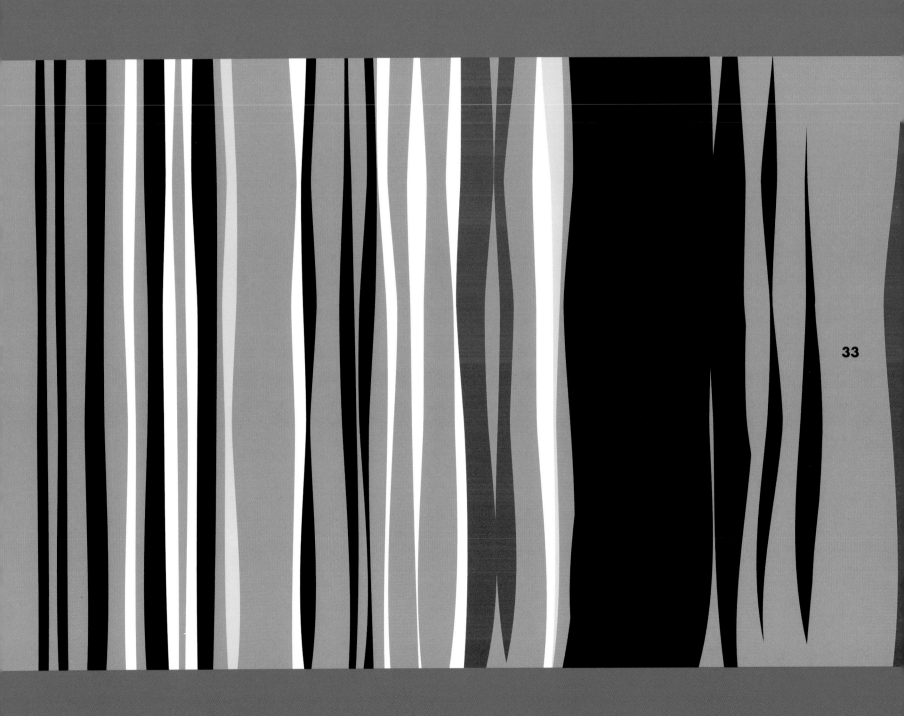

33

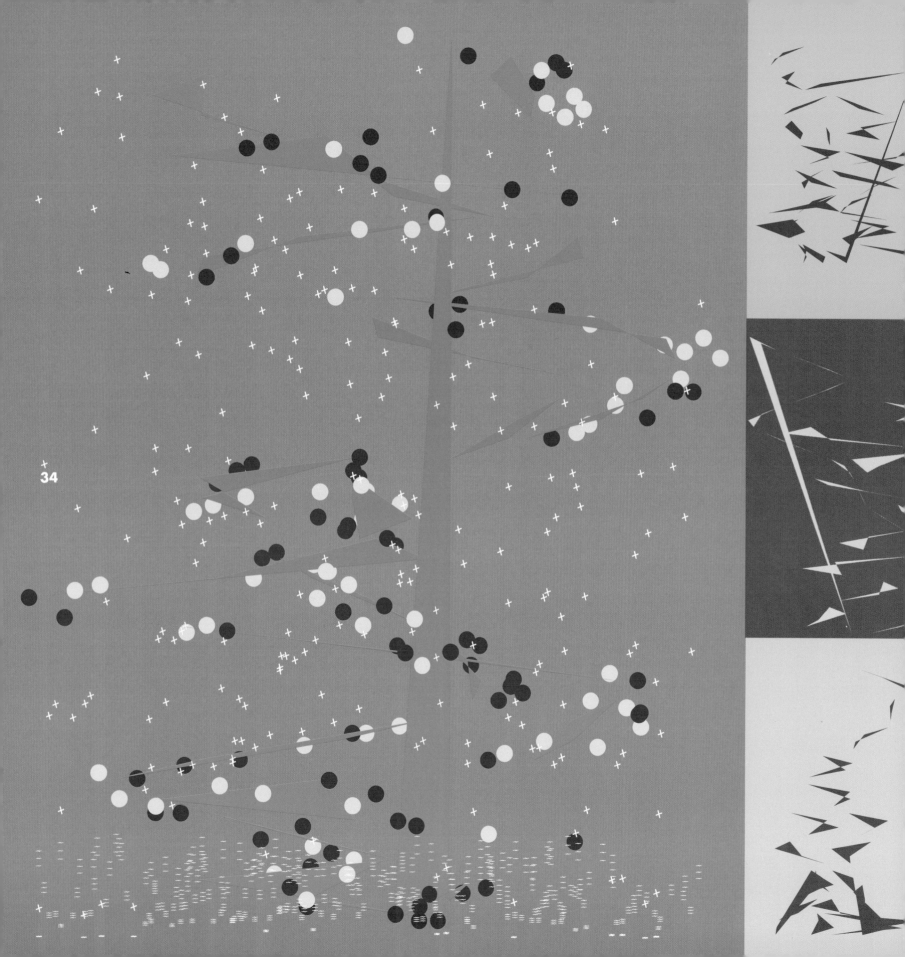

34

35

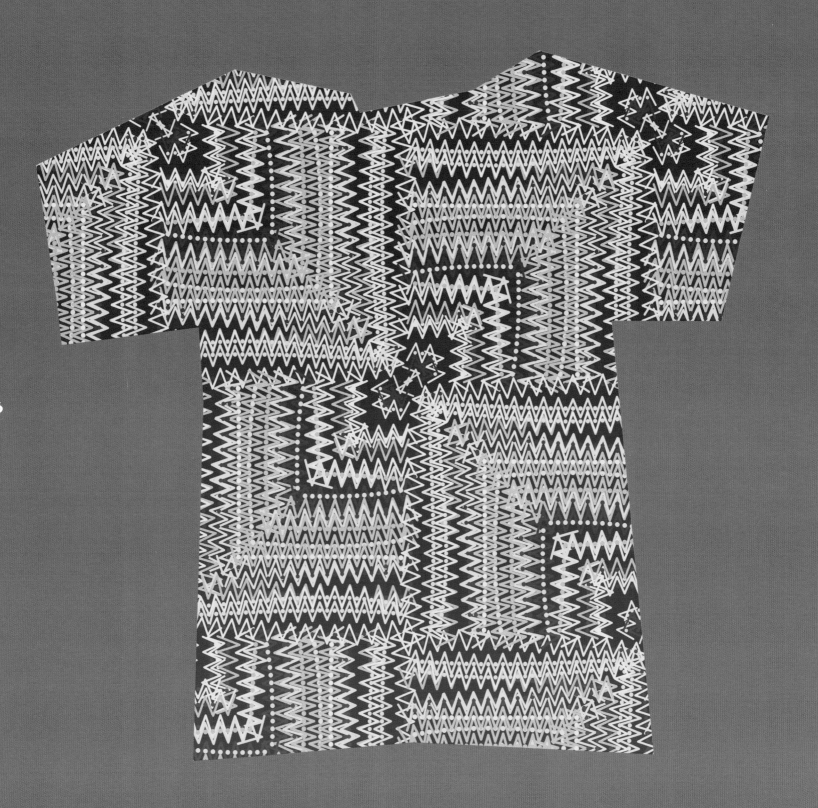

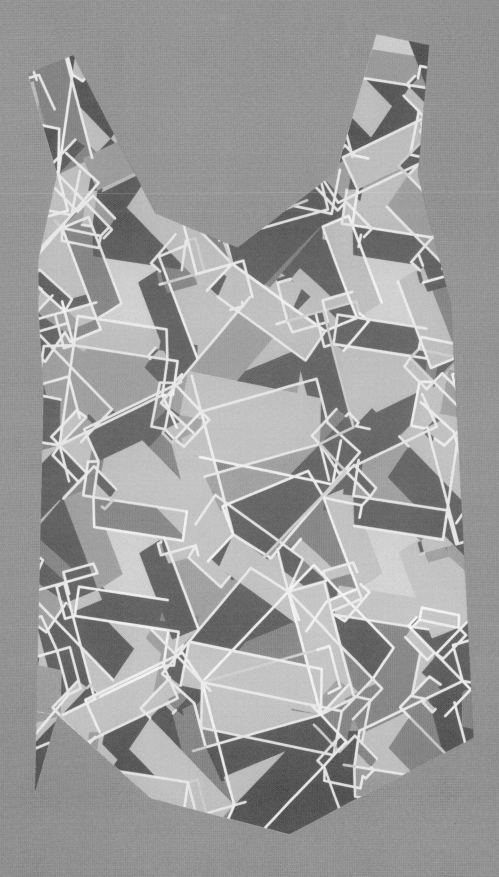

38

39

40

42

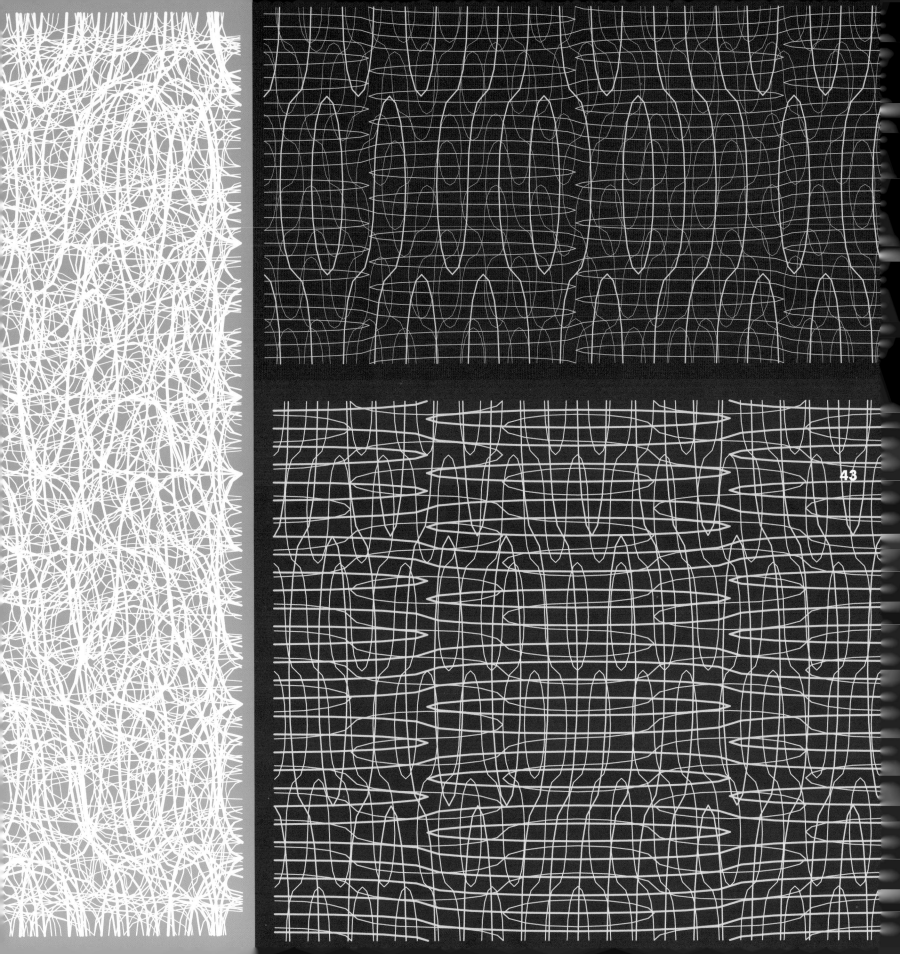

43

45

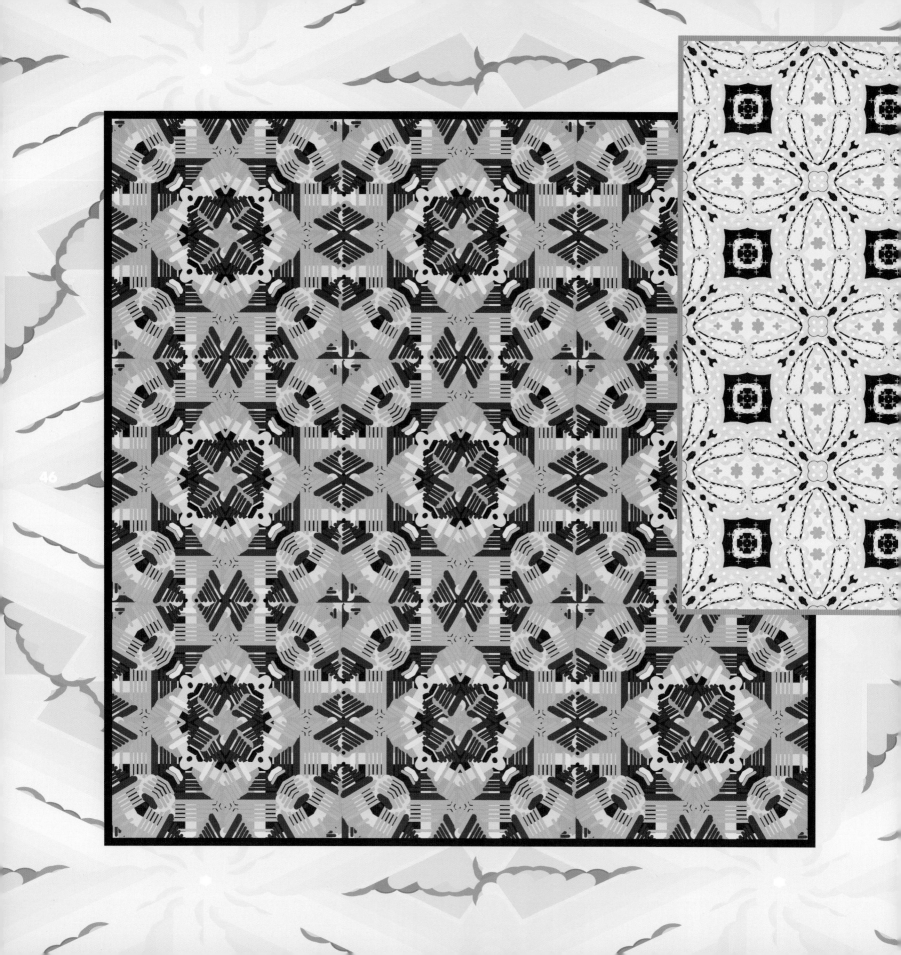

50

51

52

54

55

57

58

59

60

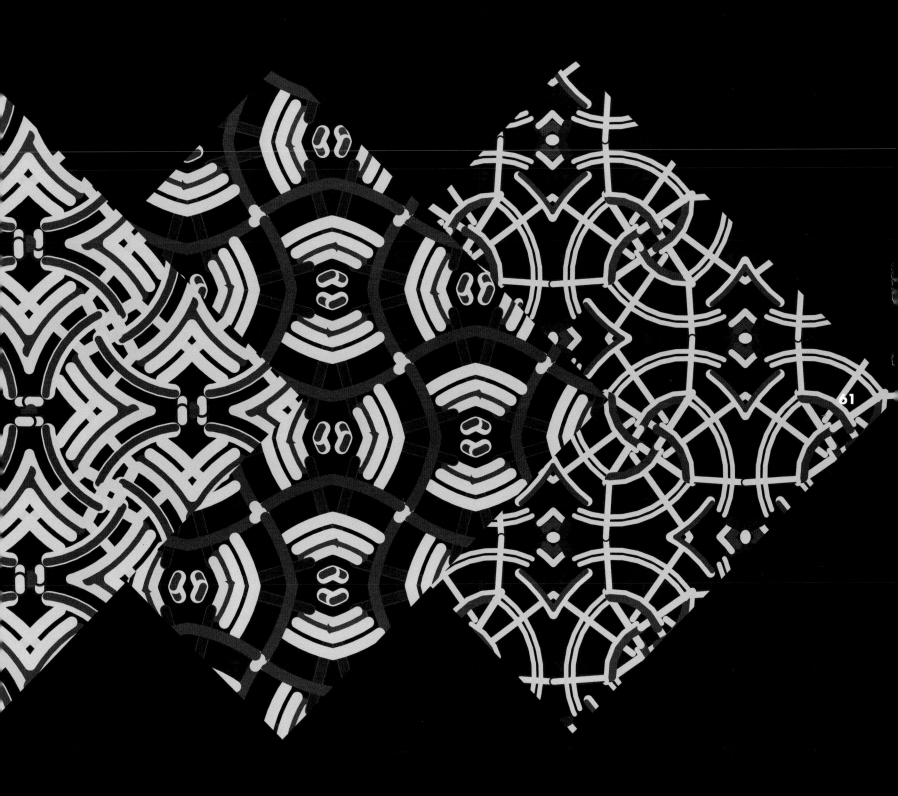

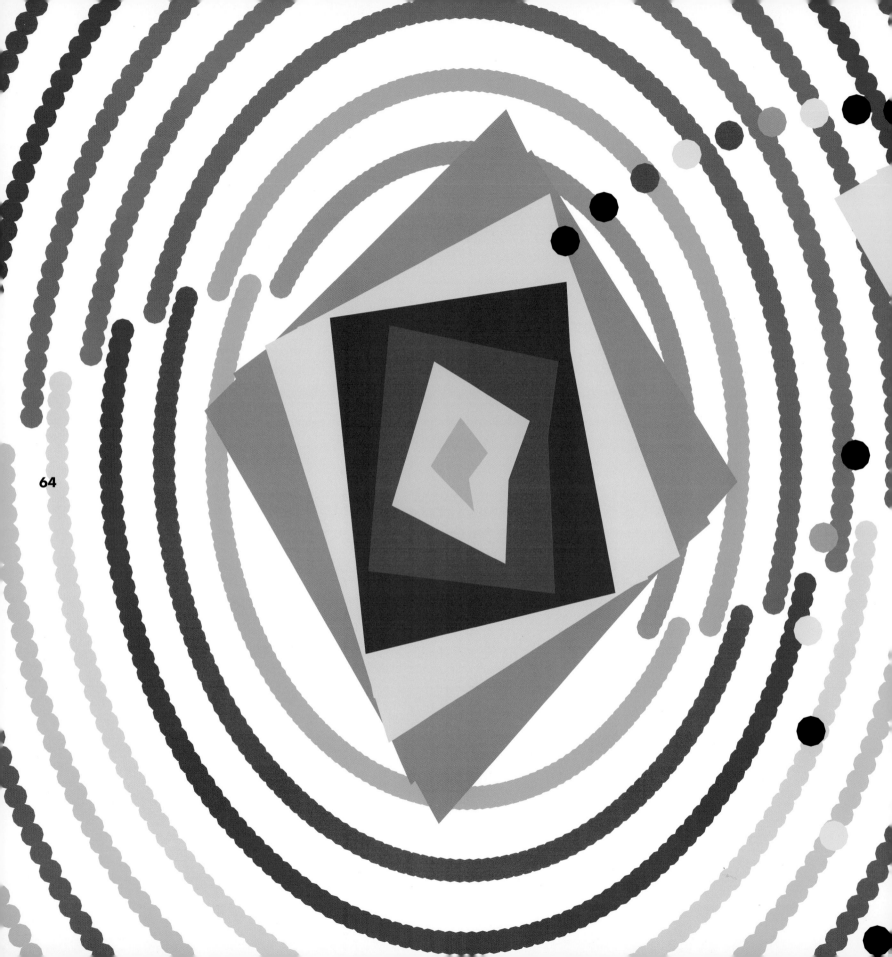

64

66

68

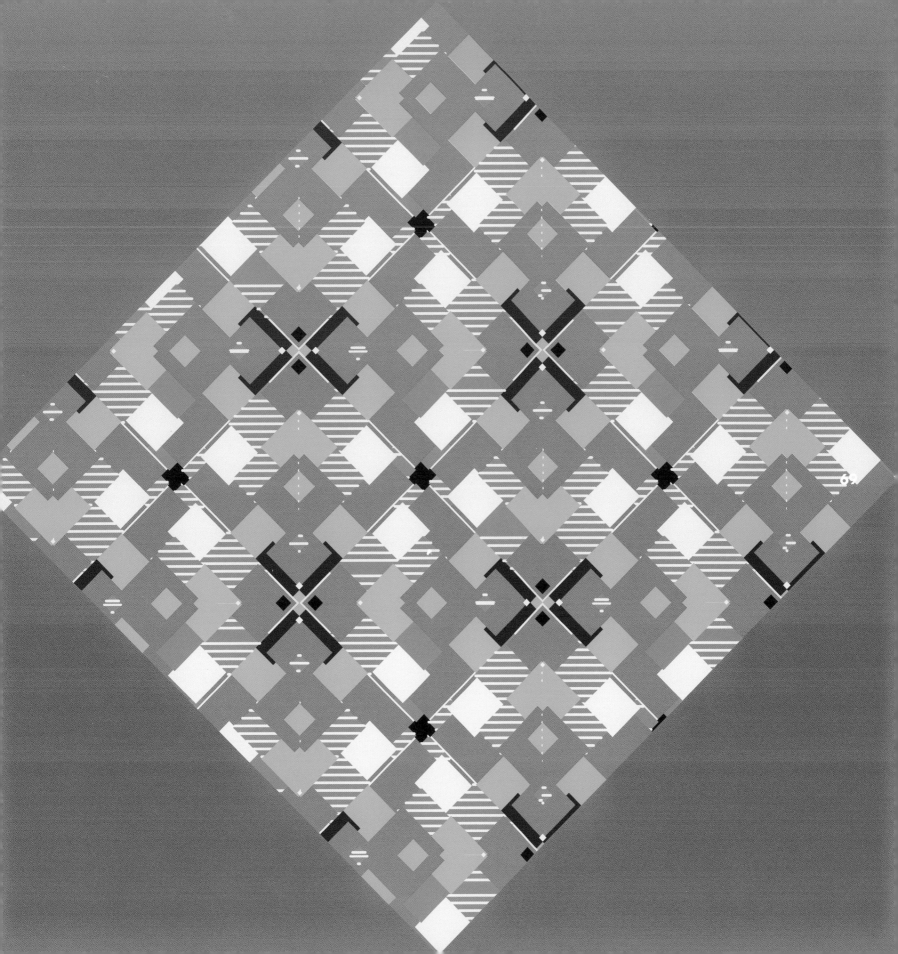

72

STEP BY STEP

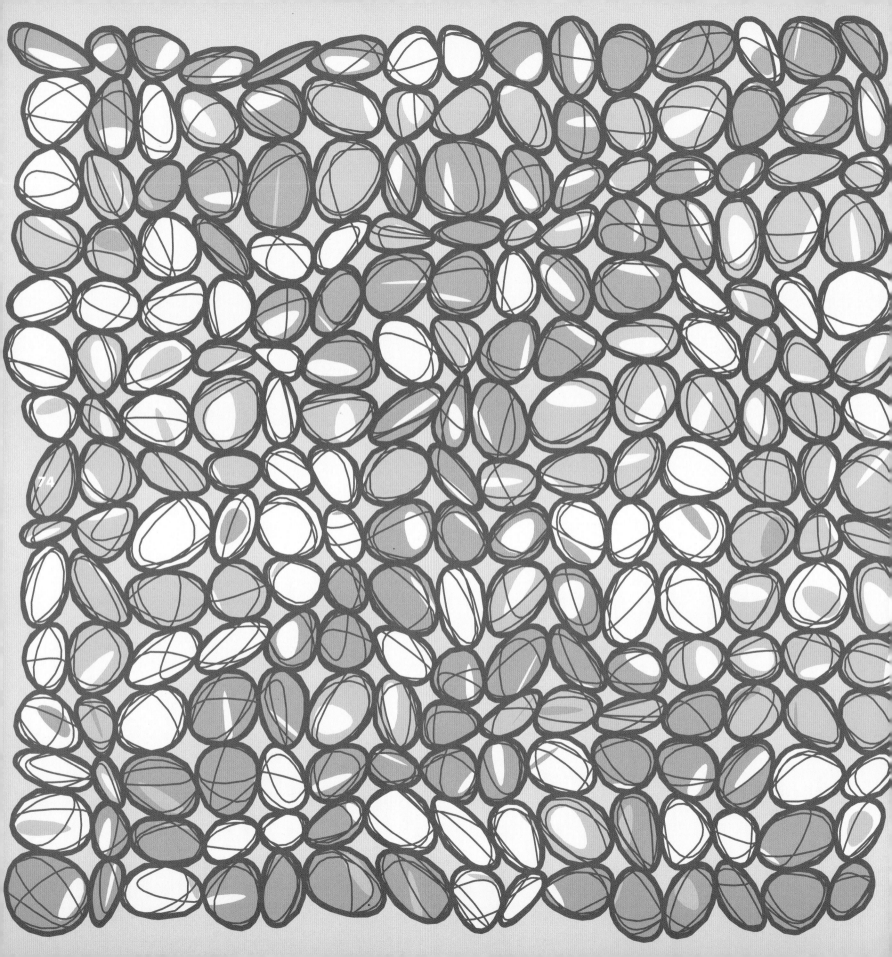

WHAT MAKES AN ATTRACTIVE IMAGE?

In the past, graphic art had to be painstakingly created from individual primitives such as lines, polygons, or brush strokes. But now, with *Mathematica*, an artist can think at a higher level, creating complex objects all at once with the click of a mouse. *Mathematica* makes this possible with its ability to describe processes as well as objects. Instead of having to specify directly where each element in an image should go, an artist can specify an algorithm, and *Mathematica* can then form the final image.

Artlandia, a *Mathematica*-based application for creative graphics design, provides such tools. In this section, we use *Artlandia* to reveal the graphical character of several fundamental random processes. We will also describe how to use it, in a step-by-step fashion, to create a few images from this book.

Signatures of Randomness

Random processes play the central part in this book and in our entire approach to the artificial generation of attractive patterns. The characteristic property of a random process—or an array of random numbers—is its time or space correlation, as characterized by its power spectrum. There are three fundamental types of random processes that describe the majority of the random processes in nature: those exhibiting the flat (*i.e.*, independent of frequency f) spectrum, the flicker (or $1/f$-type) spectrum, and the random-walk (or $1/f^2$-type) spectrum.

These power spectra describe just how "random" a random sequence is. If we know that one number in the sequence has some specific value α, what constraints, statistically, are there on the next number in the sequence? In white noise sequences, there are no constraints, and all values are equally likely. In flicker sequences, there are moderate constraints making numbers near α more likely; in random-walk sequences there are even stronger contraints making numbers near α still more likely. *Artlandia* makes these arrays (in their *n*-dimensional incarnation) immediately accessible for the graphics designer as the **RandomArray**, **NaturalArray**, and **RandomWalkArray** functions. The name **NaturalArray** indicates both that the $1/f$ spectrum is the most widespread in nature and that in many cases it seems to yield the most harmonized images. In fact, **NaturalArray** is the default array for many *Artlandia* functions.

Let's familiarize ourselves with some of the tools available in *Artlandia*.

We start by loading *Artlandia*.

```
<< Artlandia`
```

In this image of 150 × 150 pixels, the color of each pixel is independent of the color of its neighbors. This is "white" noise, even though none of the individual pixels are actually white.

```
Show[Graphics[
     Raster[RandomArray[{150, 150}, {0, 1}],
   ColorFunction → Hue]], AspectRatio → Automatic];
```

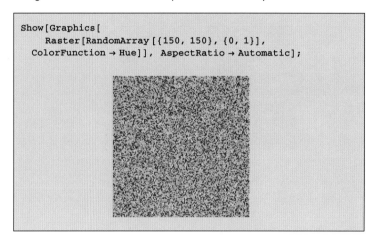

This is an example of the natural color selection ("pink" noise).

```
Show[Graphics[
     Raster[NaturalArray[{150, 150}, {0, 1}],
   ColorFunction → Hue]], AspectRatio → Automatic];
```

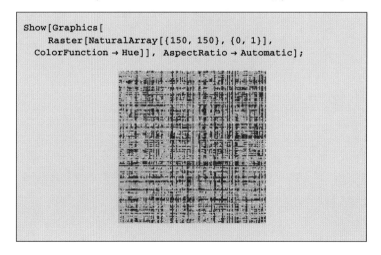

This is an example of random-walk color correlation.

```
Show[Graphics[
    Raster[RandomWalkArray[{150, 150}, {0, 1}],
    ColorFunction → Hue]], AspectRatio → Automatic];
```

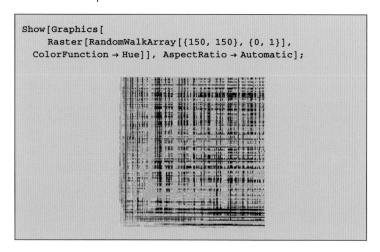

"Natural" Truchets

As a more practical illustration, we consider random Truchet patterns, those based on Sebastien Truchet's tiling (see, *e.g.*, E.H. Gombrich, *The Sense of Order.* Ithaca, New York: Cornell University Press, 1979). We will define a **Truchet** function that creates two types of tiles, each formed by a pair of quarter circles. Depending on the value of the first argument, which can be either 0 or 1, the centers of the arcs are arranged either top left and lower right or top right and lower left. The function is essentially similar to the one defined in P. Abbott, *The Mathematica Journal*, Volume 4, Issue 2 (1994), p. 25.

```
Truchet[0, {x_, y_}] :=
    {Circle[{x, y + 1}, 1/2, {-π/2, 0}],
    Circle[{x + 1, y}, 1/2, {π/2, π}]}
```

```
Truchet[1, {x_, y_}] := {Circle[{x, y}, 1/2, {0, π/2}],
    Circle[{x + 1, y + 1}, 1/2, {π, 3π/2}]}
```

Here are the two tiles.

```
Show[GraphicsArray[Graphics[Truchet[#, {0, 0}],
    AspectRatio → 1]&/@{0, 1}], GraphicsSpacing → .1];
```

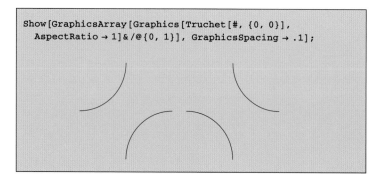

This function converts a matrix of zeros and ones into the Truchet tiling.

```
TruchetMatrix[mat_] := MapIndexed[Truchet, mat, {2}]
```

Here are the mazes brought about by the **RandomArray**, **NaturalArray**, and **RandomWalkArray** functions. Notice that the **RandomArray** maze has on average the shortest and the **RandomWalkArray** has the longest connected paths.

```
Show GraphicsArray Graphics TruchetMatrix ArrayOf
    0, 1 , 15, 15 , GeneratingFunction # ,
    AspectRatio  Automatic &
    RandomArray, NaturalArray, RandomWalkArray  ;
```

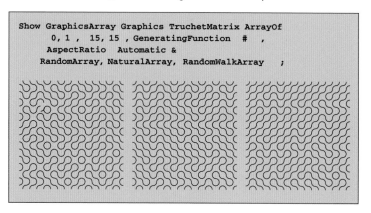

Several similar "natural" mazes of different periods, one overlaid on the other, lead to a beautiful lace image that follows. Here is the algorithm to generate a simplified lace that consists of *n* = 12 tilings. *Artlandia* users can reproduce the larger image in the book with *n* = 30.

```
n = 12;
```

76

The color palette for the pattern consists of a spectrum of *n* shades from **RGBColor[.8,1,1]** (a very light blue) to the white color. Note that, by default, the **Shades** function automatically creates the natural distribution of colors in the given color range.

```
colors = Shades[{RGBColor[.8, 1, 1], White}, n];
```

Here is the superposition of *n* tilings of different scales combined in one image; the coarser tilings are drawn with thicker lines.

```
Show[CombineGraphics[
    MapThread[Graphics[{{AbsoluteThickness[ 10. / # ],
        #2, TruchetMatrix[ArrayOf[{0, 1}, {#, #}]]},
        AspectRatio → 1, PlotRange → All]&,
        {Round[NaturalArray[n, {5, 20} ]], colors}],
    Background → CornflowerBlue, ToSameSize → Automatic],
    AspectRatio → 1];
```

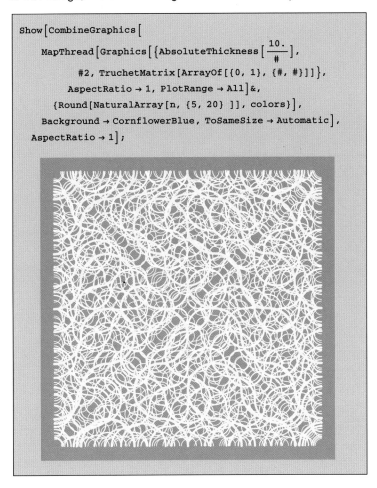

Carving the *Cellular Automata Stones*

To compute the *Cellular Automata Stones*, we start from a naturally distorted lattice, partition it into quadrilaterals, and round their corners, ending with an image of a stone wall. To paint the wall, we implement Stephen Wolfram's suggestion of using the cellular

automata rule 30. (Cellular automata, and rule 30 in particular, are described in more detail in the demonstration notebook "Cellular Automata" distributed with *Mathematica*.) Next, we finish by putting some shades and tinges on the stones to add some pleasing depth. The description of the algorithm is borrowed from *The Artlandia Guide*, in which the reader can also find the description of all *Artlandia* functions used in this and previous examples. Here, we create a small 4×7 piece of the wall; the larger image in this book is a 7×13 piece.

Setting up the Lattice

This is a set of points arranged in a square lattice. To have an array of stones of dimensions **dim**, we construct an array of points of dimensions **dim** + 1.

```
dim = {4, 7};
```

```
points = Map[Point, Lattice[dim + 1], {2}];
```

```
Show[Graphics[points]];
```

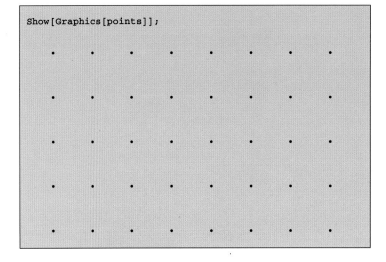

This applies the natural (flicker) distortion of the specified magnitude to the lattice.

```
points  Displace  points, .12  ;
```

```
Show[Graphics[points]];
```

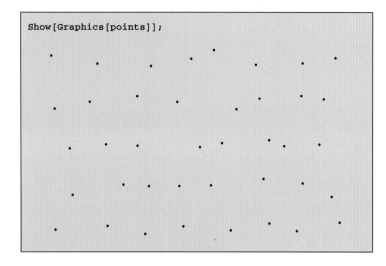

Making and Carving the Stones

The ad hoc function **Quadrilaterals** partitions a two-dimensional array of points into quartets suitable for representing the coordinates of polygons.

```
stones = Map[Polygon, Quadrilaterals[points], {2}];
```

Here is a random coloring of the resulting "stones."

```
Show[Graphics[Paint[stones, Thread[Hue[Ramp[20]]],
     GeneratingFunction → RandomArray]],
   AspectRatio → Automatic];
```

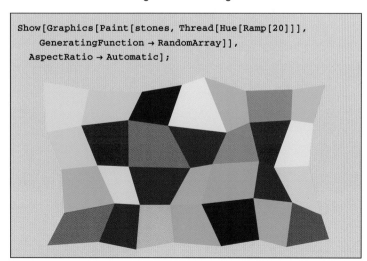

The function **RoundCorners** carves away the sharp corners of the stones.

```
stones = RoundCorners[stones];
```

This displays both the original stones and the carved ones.

```
Show[%%, Graphics[{Brown, stones}],
   AspectRatio -> Automatic];
```

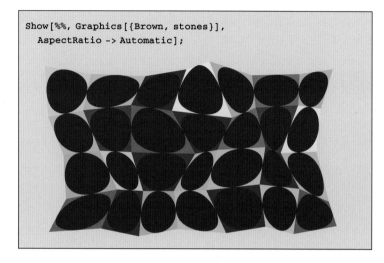

Cellular Automata Image

In the next step we use Stephen Wolfram's cellular automata code from the *Mathematica* notebook "Cellular Automata."

This sets up components for simulation of the cellular automaton system.

```
CenterList[n_Integer] := ReplacePart[Table[0, {n}], 1,
   Ceiling[n / 2]]
```

```
ElementaryRule [num_Integer]  := IntegerDigits[num, 2, 8]
```

```
CAStep[rule_List, a_List] :=
  rule[[ 8 - (RotateLeft[a] + 2 (a + 2 RotateRight[a]))]]
```

```
CAEvolveList[rule_List, init_List, t_Integer] :=
   NestList[CAStep[rule, #]&, init, t]
```

78

This computes **dim[[1]]-1** steps in the evolution of rule 30, starting from a single "1" cell.

```
evolution = CAEvolveList[ElementaryRule[30],
  CenterList[dim[[2]]], dim[[1]] - 1];
```

```
evolution // MatrixForm
```

$$\begin{pmatrix} 0 & 0 & 0 & 1 & 0 & 0 & 0 \\ 0 & 0 & 1 & 1 & 1 & 0 & 0 \\ 0 & 1 & 1 & 0 & 0 & 1 & 0 \\ 1 & 1 & 0 & 1 & 1 & 1 & 1 \end{pmatrix}$$

We will use this two-dimensional distribution to paint the wall. The stones that correspond to 1s will be given a darker color than the rest of the wall.

Color Selection

This is the dark stone color.

```
dark = AureolineYellow;
```

The lighter stones will be given one of two possible colors.

```
light = {RGBColor[1, 1, .4], LemonChiffon};
```

To paint the stones, we first create a natural distribution of light colors.

```
stonecolor = ArrayOf[light, dim];
```

Next, we apply the dark color in appropriate places.

```
stonecolor = MapAt[dark&, stonecolor,
    Position[Reverse[evolution], 1]];
```

At this stage, the image looks like this.

```
g1  Show Graphics Transpose
    stonecolor, stones , 3, 1, 2    ;
```

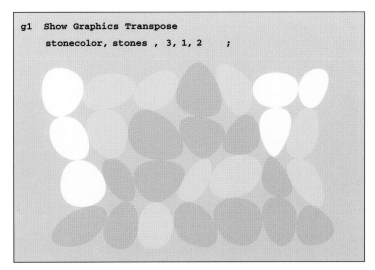

The result is, of course, still too flat and not yet interesting. We can do several things to enhance it. First, we add a distribution of small areas of color throughout the image appearing as random highlights or reflections on the stones. Next, we outline the borders of the stones using another color, creating a unifying element throughout the image. Finally, we add some tinges to the stones, again using the border color, for several reasons: to give another common element to all the stones in the wall, to make the strict borders of the stones less harsh, and to embellish the stones a bit.

This is the array of shade colors.

```
shadecolor = ArrayOf[Flatten[{light, dark}], dim];
```

To create the shades and tinges, we make a utility function that roughens the corners of each polygon in an expression by shortening the list of vertices of the polygon.

```
RoughenCorners[expr_, n_] := expr /. Polygon[poly_] :>
    Polygon[RandomElementList[poly, n]]
```

The shades on the stones are obtained by roughening the edges and rounding them again. When roughening, our utility function is set to pick up three vertices of each polygon.

```
g2 = Graphics[Transpose[{shadecolor,
    RoughenCorners[stones, 3] // RoundCorners},
  {3, 1, 2}]];
```

Here are the stones with shades.

```
Show g1, g2 ;
```

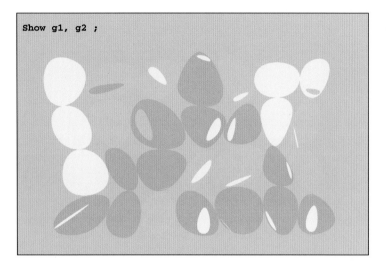

This introduces the border color.

```
border = RGBColor[.9, .3, .6];
```

This outlines the stones and shows the stones, the shades, and the borders.

```
g3 = Graphics[{border, AbsoluteThickness[3],
    stones /. Polygon → Line}];
```

```
Show g1, g2, g3 ;
```

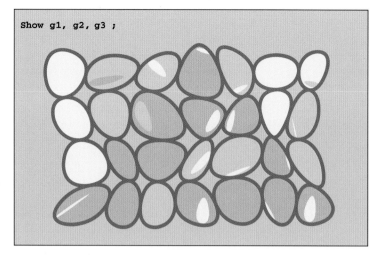

Finally the tinges are added in a manner similar to the assignment of the shades, except that in this case the roughened polygons contain eight vertices each. This makes the tinges larger and generally closer in shape to the stones.

```
g4 = Graphics[ {border, AbsoluteThickness[1],
    Table[RoughenCorners[stones, 8], {3}]} //
  RoundCorners] /. Polygon → Line;
```

```
Show g1, g2, g3, g4 ;
```

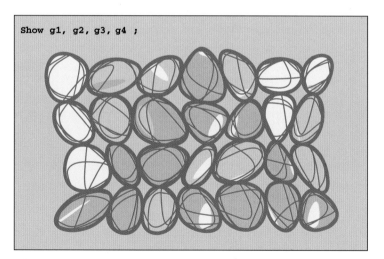

VISUAL INDEX

Most of the images in this book are literally experimental; they are the results of my experiments trying to establish the principles and techniques of creating attractive patterns by computer. The principles now form the theoretical basis and practical arsenal of *Artlandia*, a *Mathematica* application for creative graphics design.

This index describes some of my experiments, with visual references to corresponding images. It also provides hints about making these and similar images with *Artlandia*. I discuss both the fundamental built-in *Artlandia* functions and a few supplemental ad hoc *Artlandia* functions.

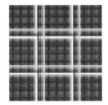

Plaid, checked, and striped patterns are long-standing favorites in applied art around us, not only because they are so easy to implement, but also because of their simple and appealing aesthetics. *Artlandia* provides functions for distributing and coloring lines, a method that easily generates surprisingly interesting plaids. Some of the plaids featured in this book were generated as wrapping paper designs for the Christmas season. **p. 5**

Converting a plaid to a check pattern is simply a matter of increasing the thickness of the lines, although another way is to specify a higher resolution—more lines per inch—with a stronger correlation between the colors of neighboring lines. Either method makes the lines merge into stripes, as in the *Lacy Check* pattern above. (For step-by-step instructions, see *The Artlandia Guide*.) **p. 6**

If we substitute narrow wedges for the straight lines in the plaid pattern and then give some random displacement to the coordinates, we can arrive at the image *Woods-in-Check*. **p. 7**

A series of stripes can be enlivened by introducing some random variations in width. In *Stripes*, left, the average width of each stripe increases linearly from left to right, and then "natural" fluctuations are introduced into each stripe.

To describe more specifically how the image is generated, an analogy might help. Imagine that this pattern were painted, giant-sized, on the side of a tall building. (This is not too unthinkable an analogy—in fact, the idea was once considered for an actual building in Japan!) To create the pattern, the painters would need to know how wide each stripe needed to be at each floor, and then they could easily paint the transition from one floor to the next. Here, the **InterpolatingArray** function calculates the widths of the stripes at each "floor" in a way that allows them to vary smoothly and gracefully as they ascend. The function **Crown** then "paints" a smooth transition from each floor to the next.

Drawing stripes is actually the simplest job for the function **Crown**, which is designed to build arbitrary shapes along arbitrary curves. More complicated shapes, like the *Grain Imitation* pattern below, arise when the basis lines are not straight. **p. 32**

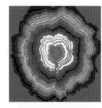

The **Periodic** option to **InterpolatingArray** is useful for turning the array into a periodic one while simultaneously smoothing it. In the *Stripes* pattern, periodicity is preserved only in the vertical direction; in other words, the top edge matches the bottom edge exactly, and the pattern can therefore be wrapped seamlessly around a cylinder. The function **PeriodicArray** can also turn any array

into a periodic one without smoothing, as shown in the pattern selected for this book's end sheets. **p. 25, end paper**

When the basis line is slanted, the resulting pattern resembles *Oblique Stripes*—something good for neckties. Color distributions similar to this one can be easily obtained using the default settings in the *Artlandia* function **Shades**. **p. 45**

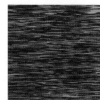

Combining stripe and plaid patterns, we can draw smooth, periodic "crowns" (using the *Artlandia* function **Crown**) along the straight line segments of a regular plaid pattern, giving images like *Violet Silk Knitwork*. **p. 45**

The *Arrows* patterns add order to random zigzags using a simple constraint: all zigzag segments must be at one of only two angles determined by the artist. **pp. 8–9, 11**

Altering the coordinates of one of the *Arrows* images using 1/f-noise displacements transforms it into *Modernistic Arrows*. **p. 10**

The *Berries* and *Exotic Summer Flowers* grow on spliced-together segments of spirals (specifically, spirals of Archimedes). The *Artlandia* function **MatchConnect** gives an easy way to match and connect curves smoothly, like the spiral segments above—although the function can also connect arbitrary graphics objects. If we add dots at the ends of the radial lines, the flowers metamorphose into *Giant Ferris Wheels*. **pp. 12–13, 44**

The petals of *Spiral Flowers* come from connecting pieces of spirals in a similar fashion. **pp. 70–71**

Mathematica gives us another way to create curves besides computing them algorithmically. We can also draw them with the mouse, as I did with the first of these *Leaves*. Once the outline was right, it was easy to choose other points along

each curve ("resample" it). Using the *Artlandia* function **Resample**, we can not only resample a curve at a fixed interval but also create clusters, for example with **NaturalArray**, as shown. **pp. 15, 19**

Different kinds of random processes—or "colored noises"—are good for different tasks. For example, "natural" or "flicker" noise would be wrong for choosing colors in these automobile upholstery designs, *Matches* and *Uprights*. Why? Because the colored noises typically create clusters, areas in a pattern in which several adjacent objects are colored so similarly that they appear as a larger single object. Such clustering keeps the pattern from having a uniform appearance at a distance. **pp. 17, 72**

On the other hand, the colored noises are indispensable when it comes to creating features within patterns, such as in this *Varilines* necktie design. Notice that the "flicker" noise which colors the lines is two-dimensional, correlating color both along each line and between the lines. *N*-dimensional "flicker" noise can be obtained with the *Artlandia* function **NaturalArray**.

The same visual effects can be overlaid on a graphic using the *Artlandia* function **Paint.** By default, **Paint** attempts to detect two-dimensional structures in a graphic and color them accordingly.

Another dimension in this design, the varying thickness of the six lines, can be added easily using the ad hoc function **CalligraphicLine**. **p. 41**

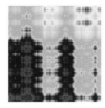

The correlation properties of the colored noises—even without much artistic intervention—can bring about interesting designs. This *Random Map* image can be generated by the *Artlandia* function **RandomWalkArray** and drawn using the built-in *Mathematica* plotting routines. **p. 45**

In these *Seam Imitation* images, the colored noises produce such effects as a worn-out robe and hand-stitching (from a decidedly unpracticed mender—perhaps an irritated bachelor!). In *Artlandia*, stitches can be created using the ad hoc function **Stitch**. **pp. 20–21**

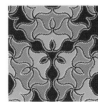

Another similar embellishment can be added with the ad hoc function **Zigzag**. **pp. 52–53**

In fact, this embellishment can grow to become the main element, as in the *Zigzags* pattern, described in *The Artlandia Guide*. **p. 36**

The colored noise is equally useful in the creation of either the natural precipitation of snow on this Christmas wrapping paper design or the playful mood of the narrow stripe hiding behind the wider one. **pp. 22–23**

Another way to tone down individual features brought about by colored noise, without ending in pure and "soulless" randomness, is to overlap several colored-noise images. We have already seen this process in the *Natural Truchets* pattern described in the previous section of this book. By such overlapping, the individual variations in each pattern are cancelled out to a degree without being eradicated. **p. 42**

84

Correlation in colored noises also comes in handy to tone down and add subtlety to images that otherwise exhibit features that are too predominant. This technique has been used, for example, to paint the background stones in the *Cellular Automata Stones*, as described in detail in the previous section. **end paper design**

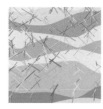

In this *Smeared Stripes* pattern, similarly to the *Cellular Automata Stones*, an additional random effect is used to soften the strict borders in an image. **p. 38**

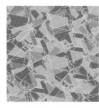

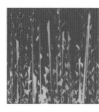

Still further, the borders can be outlined, bringing forward the common element throughout the image. **pp. 37, 39**

Because we are manipulating data, we can subject design elements to more distortion or transformation than would be possible if we were twisting or bending real, physical objects. We can "over-bend the stick"—which in this case translates to "increase parameters in the algorithm far beyond reasonable limits." In this way, the *Bamboo* image arises from the stripes pattern. **p. iv**

If the distortion from "over-bending the stick" goes too far, there are plenty of ways to bring the pattern back into balance. One way is the addition of symmetry, as in this *Rosettes* pattern. (For a step-by-step description, see *The Artlandia Guide*.) **p. 47**

The *Artlandia* function **ContourTransition** is useful in creating non-traditional gradients between arbitrary contours or curves, such as the ones that appear in the design *Liquidambar Styraciflua Leaf.* **p. 18**

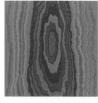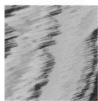

A more involved kind of transition is featured in the *Grain Imitation* patterns and related fabric designs. The intricate forms in these patterns arise from the superposition of random processes of different magnitude and characteristic correlation times, including the so-called "burst noise." (The same effect can be seen as electrical noise within physical devices like a transistor or a thin metal film.) The burst noise can easily be generated using the ad hoc function **Bursts**.

Once the raw array of heights of individual contours are created, the correlation between the neighboring contours can be added. This process is a simple model of the growth of a tree trunk, which takes years (and corresponding layers of grain) to heal some of the bigger variances. Then, it's straightforward to turn the array of numbers into the coordinates of grains or oblique stripes using the *Artlandia* function **Crown** mentioned earlier. **pp. 24–25**

Many designs originate from repeating a motif on a lattice grid. In *Artlandia*, such grids can be obtained using the function **Lattice**. Although **Lattice** by default generates a square grid, others—and not just rectangular ones—can be obtained with the same ease. The *Eyed Balls* patterns above, for example, use a rhomboidal lattice. **p. 44**

These images are collectively titled *The Archimedes' Spirals—in Wine and Arctic Sea*. Each figure is built using two color gradients, one for the spirals and an opposing gradient for the background stripes. Archemedean spirals, generated with the default settings of the function **Spiral**, are among many types of ready-made curves available in *Artlandia*. The top picture was first published on the cover of Toshimitsu Musha's *Novel Ideas Coming from the Concept of Fluctuations*, NHK, 1993 (in Japanese). **pp. 2–3**

In *Connections*, random semi-ellipses are connected and interwoven to form a texture with industrial overtones—or social overtones, if you take the image as a representation of the tight interconnection between the various sectors of society. **pp. 50**

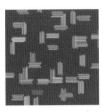

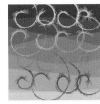

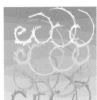

The underlying grid itself can be distorted, among other ways, with the function **Displace**. The motifs for *Snails* and *Strokes* patterns are obtained using the ad hoc functions **Snail** and **Stroke**. A "snail" is a collection of almost concentric disks, and a "stroke" is a superposition of parallel lines with a specified distribution of start and end points. **pp. 26, 29**

Just as in the preceding images, these *Snowy Spirographs* are built of a series of short lines tangent to the underlying curve. Another visual dimension has been added by coloring the lines using a "natural" color distribution obtainable through the function **Shades**. **pp. 48–49**

Building objects using polar coordinates—constructed using the *Artlandia* function **PolarList**—is another way of visualizing the statistical properties of arrays of numbers. *Hedgehogs* like these, for example, can be obtained by transforming vectors generated with **NaturalArray** into a collection of teardrop-shaped regions sharing a common origin. (I call this process "polarizing," since it involves polar coordinates.) Each teardrop has two parameters: angular width, and the shape of the outer curve. **pp. 44, 56–57**

85

The **Stroke** function is also in the origin of the *Mosaic Strokes* pattern—described in detail in *The Artlandia Guide*—and its derivatives. **pp. 58–59**

The curve-generating functions in *Artlandia* take the option **PlotPoints**, letting the user control the amount of detail to be used when generating the curve. Normally this option is used to make sure that the curves being plotted are drawn smoothly. However, interesting effects can be created by setting **PlotPoints** to a value intentionally too low to produce a smooth curve, as in the *Summer Spirals* images. **p. 64**

This image, *Random Butterflies on Random Lattice*, can be created by creating random vectors, smoothing them using the **InterpolatingArray** filter, "polarizing" them, and then overlaying the result on top of "strokes" created with the **Stroke** function. **pp. 54–55**

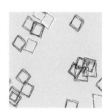

The random component in the lattice distortion can be increased until it completely overwhelms the regular component, as in this *Multisquares* image. **p. 44**

It is a simple matter to add slanted lines to an image and create *The Effect of Rain*. Additionally, *Artlandia* allows you to fill shapes or contours with a hatching pattern, as in this traditional Japanese *Sippo-Tsunagi* pattern and in the *Squares* pattern. *The Artlandia Guide* gives the step-by-step instructions for creating both. **pp. 31, 45, 69**

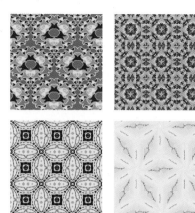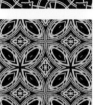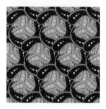

Besides the means to control the random distribution of elements throughout the image, *Artlandia* provides functions that convert planar graphical objects into symmetrically repeating patterns. There are seventeen possible symmetries, and even mathematicians often refer to them as "wallpaper groups" because such patterns repeat like a wallpaper print. In each symmetry, a basic unit cell is repeated—sometimes rotated or in mirror image—in a regular way. **pp. 45–46**

The ability to add symmetries to an image can make the designer very productive, allowing the generation of a host of graphics in a matter of minutes. **pp. 61, 63**

As this *Paisleys* pattern shows, the smallest basic cells of a tiling in *Artlandia* need not all be identical. *Artlandia* can combine different unit cells to create a tile or different tiles to create a tiling, giving the designer even greater flexibility. **p. 47**